This or That

Questions
About the
Wilderness
You Decide!

by Jaclyn Jaycox

Raintree is an imprint of Capstone Global Library Limited, a company incorporated in England and Wales having its registered office at 264 Banbury Road, Oxford, OX2 7DY – Registered company number: 6695582

www.raintree.co.uk
myorders@raintree.co.uk

Edited by Gena Chester
Designed by Heidi Thompson
Original illustrations © Capstone Global Librar
Picture research by Jo Miller
Production by Tori Abraham
Originated by Capstone Global Library Ltd

978 1 3982 3461 1 (hardback)
978 1 3982 3462 8 (paperback)

British Library Cataloguing in Publication Da
A full catalogue record for this book is available

Acknowledgements
We would like to thank the following for permission to reproduce photographs: Shutterstock: aaltair, 26, Alberto Menendez Cervero, 15, Anan Kaewkhammul, Cover (puma), Antoni Murcia, 22, AshimovSJ, 10, Billion Photos, 29, Brittany Mason, 23, Chris Galkowski, 18, Coppee Audrey, 12, cunaplus, 11, Dawn Balaban, 25, Dennis W Donohue, Cover (bear), everydaytextures, 14, Gallinago_media, Cover (moose), Galyna Andrushko, Cover (landscape), Hans Verburg, 24, HTurner, 9, John Corry, 13, Kelly vanDellen, 19, kosmos111, 21, lzf, 16, maphke, 3, Maridav, 20, Michaela Mazurkova, 7, NatalieJean, 8, Northof60Girl, 6, Prostock-studio, 17, Roman Mikhailiuk, 27, Virrage Images, 28, Volodymyr Martyniuk, 4. Design element: Shutterstock: Morphart Creation, Cover (map).

Every effort has been made to contact copyright holders of material reproduced in this book. Any omissions will be rectified in subsequent printings if notice is given to the publisher.

All the internet addresses (URLs) given in this book were valid at the time of going to press. However, due to the dynamic nature of the internet, some addresses may have changed, or sites may have changed or ceased to exist since publication. While the author and publisher regret any inconvenience this may cause readers, no responsibility for any such changes can be accepted by either the author or the publisher.

About the wilderness

Imagine you are on a hiking trip in the wilderness. After a few hours, you realize you've taken a wrong turn. You aren't sure where you are. You try to find your way but end up even further off the trail. You push on, trudging over the vines, roots and bushes at your feet. You notice storm clouds heading your way. It's almost dark, and you are lost.

This situation becomes a reality for thousands of people every year. Many people enjoy exploring the outdoors, but the wilderness can be dangerous. It's home to wild animals. Severe weather can strike without notice. Rough **terrain** can be deadly.

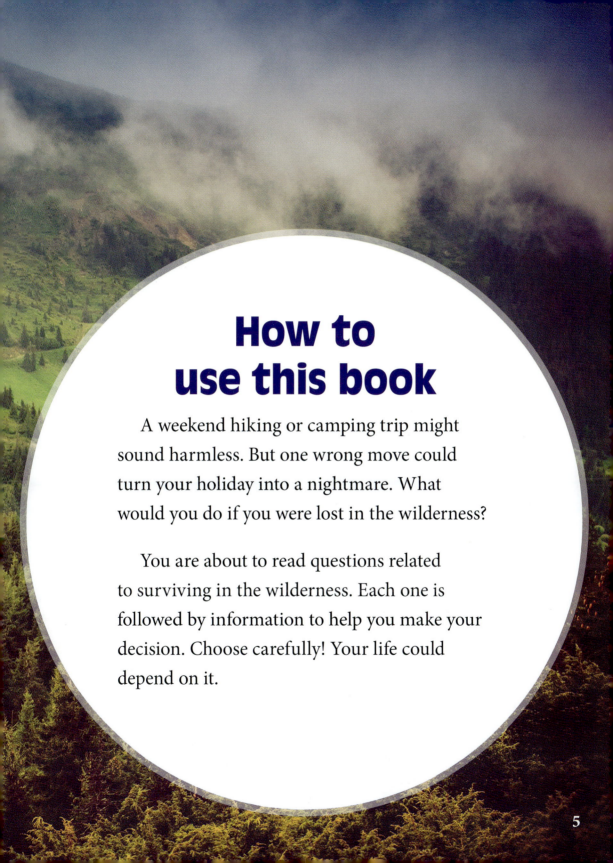

How to use this book

A weekend hiking or camping trip might sound harmless. But one wrong move could turn your holiday into a nightmare. What would you do if you were lost in the wilderness?

You are about to read questions related to surviving in the wilderness. Each one is followed by information to help you make your decision. Choose carefully! Your life could depend on it.

- ✓ explore mountains and rivers
- ✓ may run into bears
- ✓ long way from help

The Yukon is located in northwest Canada. Summers there are hot and winters can get bitterly cold. You'll find mountains, rivers and lots of wildlife. The Yukon is known as "bear country". You may run into a grizzly or black bears! Most of the Yukon is outside of mobile phone range. So it may be hard to get help if you need it.

- ✓ explore wetlands, rivers and rainforests
- ✓ heavy rains cause flooding
- ✓ crocodile-filled rivers

Kakadu National Park is found in the Northern Territory in Australia. It is hot year-round. The park contains wetlands, rivers and rainforests. From December to March, **monsoon** season hits the park. Heavy rains can cause flash floods, cutting off exits for visitors. The rivers are home to crocodiles. These animals have been known to attack humans in boats.

✓ explore the desert

✓ extreme heat and cold

✓ home to many dangerous animals

Joshua Tree National Park is found in California, USA. In this area, the Colorado Desert and Mojave Desert meet. The summers are extremely hot, and winter temperatures can drop below freezing. Sudden rainstorms can create flash floods. The park is also home to **venomous** animals such as rattlesnakes, scorpions and black widow spiders.

That?

explore
Olympic National Park

- ✓ explore many types of landscapes
- ✓ rising tides can flood trails
- ✓ risk of attacks by wild animals

Olympic National Park is found in the state of Washington, USA. This park contains many different terrains. There are rainforests, mountains, glaciers and beaches. With so many landscapes to explore, it's a hiker's paradise. But there are also dangers. Rising **tides** can cut off trails. Wild animals such as bears and mountain goats have attacked visitors who got too close.

✔ freezing temperatures

✔ risk of hypothermia

✔ dress in layers

Cool air can be refreshing. But being unprepared for the cold can put you at risk of **hypothermia**. This is when the body temperature drops. The heart and other **organs** can't work properly. It can be deadly. So it'll be important to bundle up. Dress in layers to trap in body heat and keep yourself warm. Use a waterproof outer layer to stay dry on your snowy trip.

✔ lots of sweating

✔ risk of dehydration and heatstroke

✔ take breaks

Be ready to sweat! Sweating is the body's way of cooling off. But spending too much time in the heat without drinking water can make you **dehydrated**. The body can no longer sweat to cool down. **Heatstroke** happens when your body temperature rises. It can be deadly. You'll need to beat the heat by wearing light, loose clothing. Take breaks during your hike.

✓ falling chunks of snow and ice

✓ can travel faster than cars on a motorway

✓ risk of being buried

Avalanches are masses of snow falling down a mountain. Some avalanches are small with fluffy snow sliding down. But others can be big chunks of snow and ice that break off the side of a mountain. Avalanches can travel at speeds of more than 160 km (10 miles) per hour. If you are caught in a large avalanche, you could quickly become buried.

- ✓ looks solid but acts like liquid
- ✓ almost impossible for your whole body to sink
- ✓ limbs can get stuck

DANGER
QUICKSAND

No Public Right of Way

Quicksand is a mixture of water and sand or clay. It is usually found on beaches and in valleys and stream beds. Although the ground might look solid, it will act like a liquid. Your feet will sink into it. It's nearly impossible to sink completely into quicksand. But your limbs can become stuck, making it hard to get out on your own.

- ✔ risk of heatstroke
- ✔ lack of water
- ✔ dangerous desert animals

Deserts are some of the hottest places in the world. They are also the driest. Being lost in the desert can be deadly. Water can be extremely hard to find. Without water, your body becomes dehydrated. The temperatures at night can get bitterly cold. Without shelter, you are at risk of **frostbite**. And one wrong step could result in a snakebite or scorpion sting.

- ✔ frequent thunderstorms with lightning
- ✔ risk of avalanche
- ✔ dangerous mountain animals

The mountains are beautiful, but they can be unforgiving. Depending on where you are, afternoon thunderstorms may be common. Watch out for lightning strikes! Chilly, snow-covered mountains bring the risk of hypothermia. Avalanches can bury you under snow. Lots of animals live in the mountains. Bears and mountain lions have been known to attack humans.

- ✓ available on most mobile phones
- ✓ updated often
- ✓ relies on phone signal and battery

When travelling in the wilderness, a map is a must-have. Most mobile phones have apps with electronic maps. They are updated much more often than printed maps. But many electronic maps won't work if you don't have a phone signal. And if you become lost and your phone battery dies, you will be without a map.

- ✔ no need for phone signal or batteries
- ✔ updated less often
- ✔ could be lost or ruined by weather

Paper maps can be a reliable option because they don't require phone signal or batteries. But they may not give you the most up-to-date information. A sudden gust of wind could steal a map right out of your hands. And if your map isn't waterproof, a rainstorm could make it unreadable.

- ✔ markers direct hikers
- ✔ may not be the fastest path
- ✔ markers can be removed or damaged

Official hiking trails have markers. They mark the beginning and end of trails and any direction changes. Marked trails aren't always the quickest way to go, but they usually avoid rough terrain. Markers help you stay on the correct path. But this doesn't guarantee you won't get lost. Markers can be removed by people or damaged by bad weather.

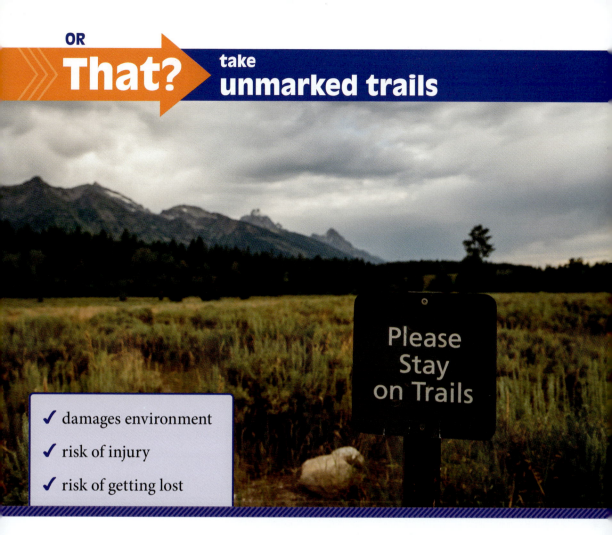

Please
Stay
on Trails

✔ damages environment

✔ risk of injury

✔ risk of getting lost

Responsible hikers avoid going off marked trails. Leaving the path can damage the natural environment. You could injure yourself on rough ground. But what if you have misjudged how long a hike will take? A short-cut might save time. It could keep you from being stuck in the woods overnight. Or, you could end up lost and many kilometres away from the correct path.

✔ protects from bad weather

✔ keeps you dry

✔ time consuming

Setting up a good, sturdy shelter is important if you are staying in the wilderness overnight. It will protect you from bad weather. Staying dry in cold temperatures is critical to your survival. But building a shelter can take time. If you are shivering, that will probably slow you down.

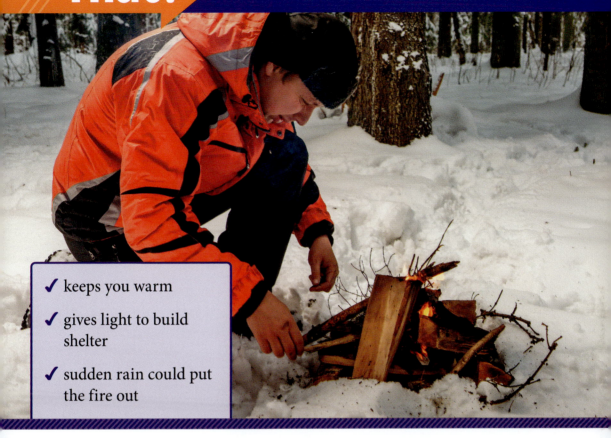

- ✔ keeps you warm
- ✔ gives light to build shelter
- ✔ sudden rain could put the fire out

The warmth of a fire could mean the difference between life and death. The flames could also light up the area enough to build your shelter. But you'll be exposed while you start the fire. And if you don't have enough supplies close by, you will have to search the woods to find them. Once you've started a fire, a sudden rainstorm could put it out.

Would You Choose
This
cross paths with
a grizzly bear

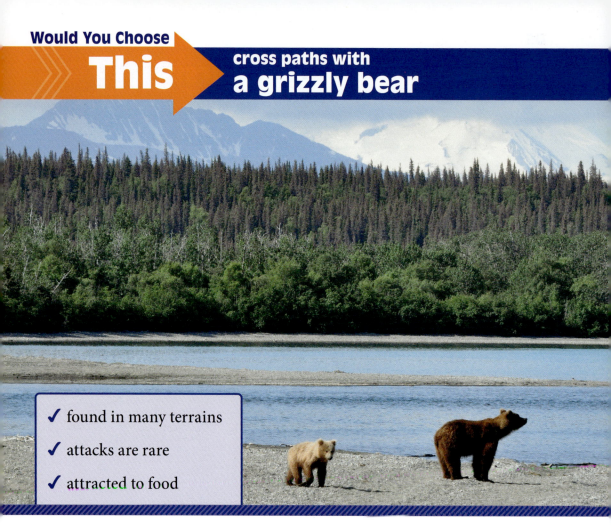

✔ found in many terrains

✔ attacks are rare

✔ attracted to food

Grizzly bears are found in North America. They live in forests, mountains and grassy plains. Every year, millions of people visit parks where grizzly bears live. Attacks on humans are rare, but they have happened. Mothers protecting their cubs have attacked people. Grizzlies are also known for sniffing out and stealing food from campsites!

- ✓ venomous
- ✓ may be hard to spot on the ground
- ✓ bites need immediate medical attention

Rattlesnakes live in North, South and Central America. These venomous animals can be found in deserts, swamps, forests and grasslands. They try to escape if they sense danger, so watch where you walk! Many rattlesnake bites happen when people step on the animals. As long as you are able to get medical help fast, their bites are usually not deadly.

- ✔ easy to find
- ✔ good source of protein
- ✔ some can make you ill

Food options are limited in the wilderness. You may have to snack on some creepy-crawlies! Insects are usually pretty easy to find. They are a great source of **protein**, which will help keep you feeling full. But be careful which insects you choose. Some types of caterpillars can make you really sick. Trying to catch a bee or a scorpion could result in a sting.

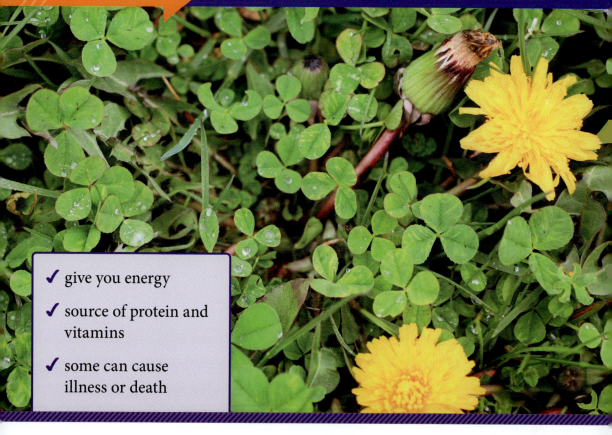

OR That? eat plants

- ✔ give you energy
- ✔ source of protein and vitamins
- ✔ some can cause illness or death

There are many plants in the wilderness that you can eat. They can give you the energy needed to survive. Dandelions are full of vitamins. Clover is rich in protein. But just like insects, you must be very careful when choosing which plants to eat. Some are poisonous. Eating the wrong type of plant could lead to severe illness or even death.

- ✔ easy to get lost
- ✔ can last several hours to days
- ✔ risk of frostbite or hypothermia

Blizzards are snowstorms. They bring strong winds of more than 56 km (35 miles) per hour. Blizzards can cause whiteout conditions, making it easy to lose your way. They can sometimes last for hours or even days. These storms usually include freezing temperatures. You could be at risk of frostbite or hypothermia.

- ✓ risk of being struck by lightning
- ✓ creeks and streams can flood
- ✓ wind can knock down trees

Thunderstorms can produce strong winds and lots of rain. Dangerous lightning also comes with these storms. Without shelter, you could be at risk of hypothermia. Small creeks and streams can flood from heavy downpours. Big gusts of wind can knock you over. They can also take down trees or blow **debris** around.

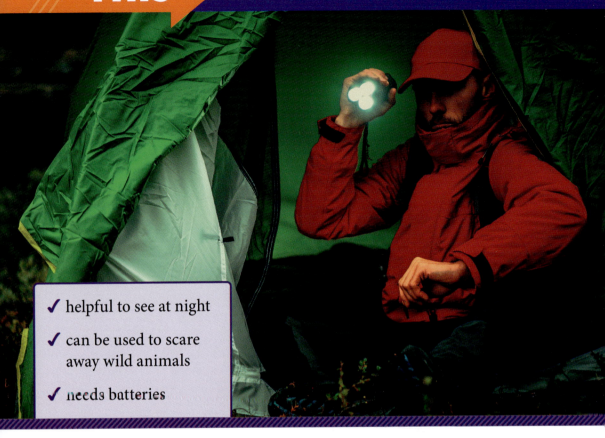

- ✓ helpful to see at night
- ✓ can be used to scare away wild animals
- ✓ needs batteries

A torch is a handy tool if you get caught in the wilderness at night. The light makes it easier to see trail markers. It can also help you spot any hazards in your path. You could avoid trips and falls that might leave you injured. A torch can also be used to scare away or fight off wild animals. Just make sure you pack spare batteries!

OR That? **have a whistle**

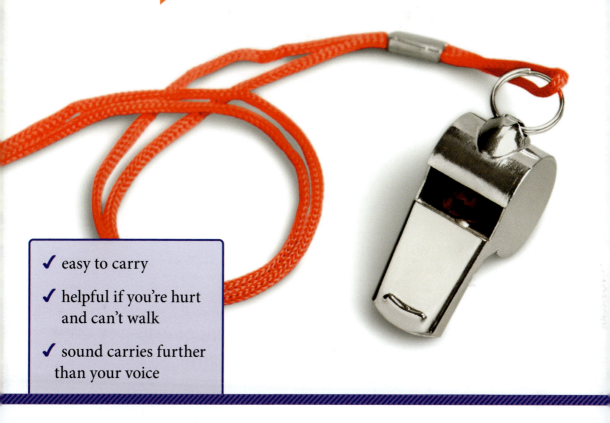

✔ easy to carry

✔ helpful if you're hurt and can't walk

✔ sound carries further than your voice

A whistle can be very useful in a survival situation. It's small and light, so you can carry it in your pocket. If you are hurt and unable to move, a whistle may be your best chance of getting help. Its sound carries further than your voice. A good survival whistle can be heard up to 1.6 km (1 mile) away.

Lightning round

Would you choose to . . .

- explore alone **or** in a group?

- have a pocketknife **or** a box of matches?

- build your own shelter **or** find a cave?

- carry 19 litres of water **or** drink from a stream?

- see a moose **or** a wolf?

- eat unknown berries **or** go without food?

- climb a mountain **or** hike down a canyon?

Glossary

debris pieces of something that has been broken apart

dehydration not having enough water

frostbite condition that happens when cold temperatures freeze skin

heatstroke life-threatening condition that happens when a person's temperature is too high and the body has lost its ability to sweat and control its temperature

hypothermia life-threatening condition that happens when a person's temperature is too low and the body is losing heat faster than it can produce it

monsoon very strong seasonal wind that brings heavy rains or hot, dry weather

organ part of the body that does a particular job; your heart, lungs and kidneys are organs

protein substance found in foods such as meat, cheese, eggs and fish that is an important part of a person's diet

terrain surface of the land

tide daily rising and falling of the ocean level

venomous able to produce a poison called venom

Find out more

Books

Amazing Human Feats of Survival (Superhuman Feats),
Annette Gulati (Raintree, 2020)

Can You Survive the Wilderness? (You Choose: Survival),
Matt Doeden (Raintree, 2014)

*Survival for Beginners: A step-by-step guide to camping and
outdoor skills*, Colin Towell (DK Children, 2019)

Surviving the Wilderness (Extreme Survival),
Michael Hurley (Raintree, 2011)

Websites

www.bbc.co.uk/bitesize/clips/z6mb4wx
Learn more about wild camping.

www.dkfindout.com/uk/earth/deserts
Find out more about deserts.